HEALING WORDS

100 SCRIPTURES *and* AFFIRMATIONS FOR WHOLENESS

SALLIE DAWKINS

Healing Words: 100 Scriptures and Affirmations for Wholeness

Library of Congress Control Number: 2023913389
ISBN: 978-1-955861-53-3 Print Paperback

Published by
Firebrand United LLC
216 Skywatch Drive #206
Danville, Kentucky
40422 USA
www.FirebrandUnited.com

CONTENTS

How to Use This Resource

Healing Words: 100 Scriptures and Affirmations for Wholeness is an excellent introductory guide for anyone wondering if God still heals.

God talks about healing in the Old and New Testaments of the Bible. His word actively declares and reveals His lovingkindness.

This book contains Bible verses about healing from the King James (KJV) translation. You'll find a paraphrased affirmation in the box above each scripture.

Affirmations provide a way to reinforce our faith, remember God's promises, and cultivate a positive mindset rooted in God's love and grace. Affirmations appeal to a wide range of people, including pre-Christians and new Christians. This guide is a great tool for healing ministry or evangelism outreach.

I encourage you to highlight these verses in your Bible or write them down. This will help you remember God's words.

Read them in context for greater understanding. Some verses might challenge your beliefs, but others will comfort you. Focusing on scripture shifts our gaze to God. I pray this book opens the door to continued conversation with God and that you grow from the experience.

Receiving God's word as truth changed my entire outlook on life. I'm learning whether instant or progressive, God still heals.

Extend your learning by referencing the scriptures and affirmations to create declarations of faith. Declarations differ from affirmations in that they're God-focused. We can easily pull scripture into our circumstances, declaring, "God is; God can; God will; God does; or God has," all according to His Word. Declarations are authoritative proclamations of faith, decreeing God's truth and power over a situation.

I extend God's love and grace to you and pray that you'll experience healing in your spirit, soul (mind, will, emotions), and body, in Jesus' name.

Your sister in Christ,

Sallie Dawkins

P.S. I encourage you to read the Bible to discover hundreds of additional healing scriptures not included here. My book, *God's Promises of Abundance for Healing*, is a more comprehensive resource, including 800+ healing scriptures indexed in over seventy categories.

Old Testament Scriptures

I embrace
a life of peace,
happiness, and
good health as I
grow older.

And thou shalt go to thy fathers in peace; thou shalt be buried in a good old age. (**Genesis 15:15**)

I am shielded
by the blood of
the Lamb of God.
No plague
will come to my
household.

And the blood shall be to you for a token upon the houses where ye are: and when I see the blood, I will pass over you, and the plague shall not be upon you to destroy you, when I smite the land of Egypt. (**Exodus 12:13**)

I am surrounded
by God's loving
shield of healing
and comfort.

I will put none of these diseases upon
thee, which I have brought upon the
Egyptians: for I am the Lord that healeth
thee. (**Exodus 15:26**)

I am blessed
by God.
As I serve Him,
my body is healed.

And ye shall serve the Lord your God, and he shall bless thy bread, and thy water; and I will take sickness away from the midst of thee. (**Exodus 23:25**)

I am
embraced by
God's radiant smile,
and blessed with
boundless peace.

The Lord lift up his countenance upon thee, and give thee peace. (**Numbers 6:26**)

I am healed
from all sickness
and God protects
me from any
harmful diseases.

And the LORD will take away from thee all sickness, and will put none of the evil diseases of Egypt, which thou knowest, upon thee; but will lay them upon all them that hate thee. (**Deuteronomy 7:15**)

I am loved
by the Lord,
and He turns any
curse into a
blessing for me.

Nevertheless the Lord thy God would not hearken unto Balaam; but the Lord thy God turned the curse into a blessing unto thee, because the Lord thy God loved thee. (**Deuteronomy 23:5**)

I am strong
and resilient.
With God,
I can face
today's challenges.

Thy shoes shall be iron and brass; and as thy days, so shall thy strength be. **(Deuteronomy 33:25)**

I am full of vitality and my vision shines brightly.

And Moses was an hundred and twenty years old when he died: his eye was not dim, nor his natural force abated. **(Deuteronomy 34:7)**

I am strong and
courageous,
for God is
always with me.

Have not I commanded thee? Be strong
and of a good courage; be not afraid,
neither be thou dismayed: for the LORD
thy God is with thee whithersoever thou
goest. (**Joshua 1:9**)

I am supported
and guided
by the Lord.
My steps are
steady and sure.

Thou hast enlarged my steps under me; so that my feet did not slip. (**2 Samuel 22:37**)

I am healed.
My tears are seen
by God, and He
answers my
prayers.

I have heard thy prayer, I have seen thy tears: behold, I will heal thee: on the third day thou shalt go up unto the house of the LORD. (**2 Kings 20:5**)

I am filled with the joy of the Lord.

For this day is holy unto our Lord: neither be ye sorry; for the joy of the LORD is your strength. (**Nehemiah 8:10**)

I am a precious child of God, filled with His breath of abundant life.

The spirit of God hath made me, and the breath of the Almighty hath given me life. (**Job 33:4**)

I am renewed
with vibrant health,
just like a child.

His flesh shall be fresher than a child's:
he shall return to the days of his youth.
(**Job 33:25**)

I am safe and secure in God's embrace.

I will both lay me down in peace, and sleep: for thou, Lord, only makest me dwell in safety. (**Psalm 4:8**)

I am guided
on the path of life
and find joy in
God's presence.

Thou wilt shew me the path of life: in thy presence is fulness of joy; at thy right hand there are pleasures for evermore. (**Psalm 16:11**)

I am richly
blessed by God,
and release
all fears and
worries.

Thou preparest a table before me in the presence of mine enemies: thou anointest my head with oil; my cup runneth over. (**Psalm 23:5**)

I release all pain and embrace God's healing power in every aspect of life.

Lord, my God, I prayed to you. And you healed me. (**Psalm 30:2**)

God protects me
and strengthens
my bones.

He keepeth all his bones: not one of them
is broken. (**Psalm 34:20**)

I am resilient
and lifted
by God's
supportive hand.

Though he fall, he shall not be utterly cast down: for the LORD upholdeth him with his hand. **(Psalm 37:24)**

I release my illness
and embrace the
Lord's strength.

The Lord will strengthen him upon the bed of languishing: thou wilt make all his bed in his sickness. (**Psalm 41:3**)

I may feel weak
at times, but
God is my heart's
strength and
eternal portion.

My flesh and my heart faileth: but God is the strength of my heart, and my portion for ever. (**Psalm 73:26**)

With God,
I am safe
from evil plagues.

There shall no evil befall thee, neither shall any plague come nigh thy dwelling. **(Psalm 91:10)**

I am blessed
with God's
everlasting
love and joy.

With long life will I satisfy him, and shew him my salvation. (**Psalm 91:16**)

I am forgiven
and accepted
by God.
He heals
all my diseases.

Who forgiveth all thine iniquities; who healeth all thy diseases. (**Psalm 103:3**)

I am blessed
by God's
abundance and
strength.

He brought them forth also with silver and gold: and there was not one feeble person among their tribes. (**Psalm 105:37**)

By God's Word,
I am healed
and delivered
from all harm.

He sent his word, and healed them, and delivered them from their destructions. (**Psalm 107:20**)

I will live
to tell the world
what the Lord
has done.

I shall not die, but live, and declare the works of the Lord. (**Psalm 118:17**)

I am healed,
for the Lord
opens my eyes,
lifts me up,
and loves me.

The Lord openeth the eyes of the blind: the Lord raiseth them that are bowed down: the Lord loveth the righteous. **(Psalm 146:8)**

I am healthy.
God has
healed my
wounded
heart.

He healeth the broken in heart, and bindeth up their wounds. (**Psalm 147:3**)

I follow
God's wisdom
to maintain a
healthy body.

Be not wise in thine own eyes: fear
the Lord, and depart from evil. It shall be
health to thy navel, and marrow to thy
bones. (**Proverbs 3:7-8**)

I release all fear.
I lie down
peacefully,
and have
sweet sleep.

When thou liest down, thou shalt not be afraid: yea, thou shalt lie down, and thy sleep shall be sweet. (**Proverbs 3:24**)

I have a
joyful heart.
My eyes shine
with light
and good reports
nourish my bones.

The light of the eyes rejoiceth the heart: and a good report maketh the bones fat. (**Proverbs 15:30**)

I am happy and strong in God's presence.

A merry heart doeth good like a medicine: but a broken spirit drieth the bones. (**Proverbs 17:22**)

I enjoy
the fruit of
the life-giving
words I speak.

Death and life are in the power of the tongue: and they that love it shall eat the fruit thereof. (**Proverbs 18:21**)

God's anointing destroys every yoke to bring freedom and healing.

And it shall come to pass in that day, that his burden shall be taken away from off thy shoulder, and his yoke from off thy neck, and the yoke shall be destroyed because of the anointing. (**Isaiah 10:27**)

I am healed.
My eyes see,
and
my ears hear.

Then the eyes of the blind shall be opened, and the ears of the deaf shall be unstopped. (**Isaiah 35:5**)

I leap
and sing
with joy
for all that
God has done.

Then shall the lame man leap as an hart, and the tongue of the dumb sing: for in the wilderness shall waters break out, and streams in the desert. (**Isaiah 35:6**)

I embrace God's healing power and strength.

He giveth power to the faint; and to them that have no might he increaseth strength. (**Isaiah 40:29**)

I am carried
by God's
unwavering love
in every
stage of life.

And even to your old age I am he; and even to hoar hairs will I carry you: I have made, and I will bear; even I will carry, and will deliver you. (**Isaiah 46:4**)

I release
all sorrow,
for Jesus
carried my grief
and set me free.

Surely he hath borne our griefs, and carried our sorrows: yet we did esteem him stricken, smitten of God, and afflicted. (**Isaiah 53:4**)

I release all pain,
for by Christ's
wounds,
I am healed.

But he was wounded for our transgressions, he was bruised for our iniquities: the chastisement of our peace was upon him; and with his stripes we are healed. **(Isaiah 53:5)**

I trust that
God's Word
will succeed
in doing
what He sent it
to do.

So shall my word be that goeth forth out of my mouth: it shall not return unto me void, but it shall accomplish that which I please, and it shall prosper in the thing whereto I sent it. (**Isaiah 55:11**)

I am
healed
in God's
presence.

Then shall thy light break forth as the morning, and thine health shall spring forth speedily: and thy righteousness shall go before thee; the glory of the Lord shall be thy reward. (**Isaiah 58:8**)

I am strong
and healthy,
praising God
for His
healing power.

Heal me, O Lord, and I shall be healed;
save me, and I shall be saved: for thou
art my praise. (**Jeremiah 17:14**)

I am known
by God.
The Lord restores
my health.

For I will restore health unto thee, and I will heal thee of thy wounds, saith the Lord; because they called thee an Outcast, saying, This is Zion, whom no man seeketh after. (**Jeremiah 30:17**)

I accept
God's healing,
abundant peace,
and truth.

Behold, I will bring it health and cure, and I will cure them, and will reveal unto them the abundance of peace and truth. **(Jeremiah 33:6)**

I am alive
with God's breath
and Spirit.

Thus saith the LORD GOD unto these bones; Behold, I will cause breath to enter into you, and ye shall live. (**Ezekiel 37:5**)

I embrace life, knowing God has fully restored my health.

And I will lay sinews upon you, and will bring up flesh upon you, and cover you with skin, and put breath in you, and ye shall live; and ye shall know that I am the LORD. (**Ezekiel 37:6**)

I am grateful
for God's
life-giving Spirit.

And shall put my spirit in you, and ye shall live, and I shall place you in your own land: then shall ye know that I the LORD have spoken it, and performed it, saith the LORD. (**Ezekiel 37:14**)

I seek God and find life.

For thus saith the LORD unto the house of Israel, Seek ye me, and ye shall live. **(Amos 5:4)**

I jump with joy as God's goodness brings healing.

But unto you that fear my name shall the Sun of righteousness arise with healing in his wings; and ye shall go forth, and grow up as calves of the stall. (**Malachi 4:2**)

New Testament Scriptures

I believe it is
God's will to heal
me and make me
clean.

And, behold, there came a leper and worshipped him, saying, Lord, if thou wilt, thou canst make me clean. And Jesus put forth his hand, and touched him, saying, I will; be thou clean. (**Matthew 8:2-3**)

I trust
Jesus will
heal me.

And Jesus saith unto him, I will come
and heal him. (**Matthew 8:7**)

I embrace God's healing touch.

And he touched her hand, and the fever left her: and she arose, and ministered unto them. (**Matthew 8:15**)

I am healed
by the powerful
Word of God.
I cast out
all negativity
within me.

They brought unto him many that were possessed with devils: and he cast out the spirits with his word, and healed all that were sick. (**Matthew 8:16**)

I am free from infirmities and sickness.

That it might be fulfilled which was spoken by Esaias the prophet, saying, Himself took our infirmities, and bare our sicknesses. (**Matthew 8:17**)

I am forgiven
of all my sins.
I will not let fear
paralyze me.

And Jesus seeing their faith said unto the sick of the palsy; Son, be of good cheer; thy sins be forgiven thee. **(Matthew 9:2)**

Jesus is my Great Physician.

But when Jesus heard that, he said unto them, They that be whole need not a physician, but they that are sick. **(Matthew 9:12)**

I dare to come
close to Christ,
and reach out to
Him as my Healer.

For she said within herself, If I may but
touch his garment, I shall be whole.
(**Matthew 9:21**)

I have faith
to be made well.

But Jesus turned him about, and when he saw her, he said, Daughter, be of good comfort; thy faith hath made thee whole. And the woman was made whole from that hour. (**Matthew 9:22**)

I believe
Jesus is able
to make me whole.
God restores vision
and gives sight to
the blind.

The blind men came to him: and Jesus saith unto them, Believe ye that I am able to do this? They said unto him, Yea, Lord. Then touched he their eyes, saying, According to your faith be it unto you. **(Matthew 9:28-29)**

Jesus heals every sickness and disease.

... and preaching the gospel of the kingdom, and healing every sickness and every disease among the people. **(Matthew 9:35)**

I rest
in the finished
works of Christ.

Come unto me, all ye that labour and are heavy laden, and I will give you rest. **(Matthew 11:28)**

Jesus heals all who follow Him.

But when Jesus knew it, he withdrew himself from thence: and great multitudes followed him, and he healed them all. (**Matthew 12:15**)

I am blessed
with wisdom to
understand
all I see and hear.

But blessed are your eyes, for they see: and your ears, for they hear. (**Matthew 13:16**)

I have compassion
to see others
healed.

And Jesus went forth, and saw a great multitude, and was moved with compassion toward them, and he healed their sick. (**Matthew 14:14**)

I am
a child of God.
Healing is the
children's bread.

But he answered and said, It is not meet to take the children's bread, and to cast it to dogs. (**Matthew 15:26**)

I cry out
to You, Lord.
I want to see You
and follow You.

So Jesus had compassion on them, and touched their eyes: and immediately their eyes received sight, and they followed him. (**Matthew 20:34**)

I release all pain
and embrace
God's healing.

And the blind and the lame came to him in the temple; and he healed them. **(Matthew 21:14)**

> # Jesus lifts me up and I am healed.

And he came and took her by the hand, and lifted her up; and immediately the fever left her, and she ministered unto them. (**Mark 1:31**)

I find freedom
and healing
in God's
presence.

And he healed many that were sick of divers diseases, and cast out many devils; and suffered not the devils to speak, because they knew him. (**Mark 1:34**)

I stretch out
my hand
to Jesus
and
He heals me.

And when he had looked round about on them with anger, being grieved for the hardness of their hearts, he saith unto the man, Stretch forth thine hand. And he stretched it out: and his hand was restored whole as the other. (**Mark 3:5**)

I bring my issues
to God
for healing
and restoration
of purity.

And straightway the fountain of her blood was dried up; and she felt in her body that she was healed of that plague. (**Mark 5:29**)

I bring God's
healing power
and love
to others.

And they cast out many devils, and anointed with oil many that were sick, and healed them. (**Mark 6:13**)

I trust Jesus
to open my ears
and loose my
tongue.

And he took him aside from the multitude, and put his fingers into his ears, and he spit, and touched his tongue. (**Mark 7:33**)

I see everything
clearly now.
God restores me
to the fullest.

After that he put his hands again upon
his eyes, and made him look up: and he
was restored, and saw every man clearly.
(Mark 8:25)

I have faith
to be healed
and made whole.

And Jesus said unto him, Go thy way; thy faith hath made thee whole. And immediately he received his sight, and followed Jesus in the way. (**Mark 10:52**)

I pray
in Jesus' name,
and see the sick
recover.

They shall lay hands on the sick, and they shall recover. (**Mark 16:18**)

I hear You, God, and You heal me.

But so much the more went there a fame abroad of him: and great multitudes came together to hear, and to be healed by him of their infirmities. (**Luke 5:15**)

In God's
presence,
I am fully
restored.

And looking round about upon them all, he said unto the man, Stretch forth thy hand. And he did so: and his hand was restored whole as the other. (**Luke 6:10**)

Jesus sent His word of healing.

Wherefore neither thought I myself worthy to come unto thee: but say in a word, and my servant shall be healed. (**Luke 7:7**)

I am free from all bondage and oppression, in Jesus' name.

For he had commanded the unclean spirit to come out of the man. (**Luke 8:29**)

I believe
God has
made me whole.

But when Jesus heard it, he answered him, saying, Fear not: believe only, and she shall be made whole. (**Luke 8:50**)

I hear Jesus
calling me
to rise up.
He has restored me
to a full life.

And he put them all out, and took her by
the hand, and called, saying, Maid, arise.
(**Luke 8:54**)

I find healing in God's Kingdom.

And the people, when they knew it, followed him: and he received them, and spake unto them of the kingdom of God, and healed them that had need of healing. (**Luke 9:11**)

I am saved,
healed,
and made whole
by Jesus Christ,
my Lord.

For the Son of man is not come to destroy men's lives, but to save them. (**Luke 9:56**)

I marvel
at God's handiwork
and will speak
of His love forever.

And he was casting out a devil, and it was dumb. And it came to pass, when the devil was gone out, the dumb spake; and the people wondered. (**Luke 11:14**)

God freed me
from the weight
of my infirmity.

And when Jesus saw her, he called her to him, and said unto her, Woman, thou art loosed from thine infirmity. And he laid his hands on her: and immediately she was made straight, and glorified God. **(Luke 13:12-13)**

I receive
restoration
of my vision
by faith in Christ.

And Jesus said unto him, Receive thy sight: thy faith hath saved thee. (**Luke 18:42**)

I walk in victory.
Jesus makes
me whole.

Jesus saith unto him, Rise, take up thy bed, and walk. And immediately the man was made whole, and took up his bed, and walked. (**John 5:8-9**)

In Christ, I have fullness of life.

The thief cometh not, but for to steal, and to kill, and to destroy: I am come that they might have life, and that they might have it more abundantly. (**John 10:10**)

I hear God
call my name.
He will use my life
for His glory.

When Jesus heard that, he said, This sickness is not unto death, but for the glory of God, that the Son of God might be glorified thereby. (**John 11:4**)

I arise
with joy
because
Christ has
made me whole.

And Peter said unto him, Aeneas, Jesus Christ maketh thee whole: arise, and make thy bed. And he arose immediately. (**Acts 9:34**)

God is with me.
I have the power
to do good
and heal,
in Jesus' name.

How God anointed Jesus of Nazareth with the Holy Ghost and with power: who went about doing good, and healing all that were oppressed of the devil; for God was with him. (**Acts 10:38**)

In Christ,
I am free
from the law
that brings
sin and death.

For the law of the Spirit of life in Christ Jesus hath made me free from the law of sin and death. (**Romans 8:2**)

I release
all sickness.
God's mercy heals
me and brings joy
instead of sorrow.

For indeed he was sick nigh unto death: but God had mercy on him; and not on him only, but on me also, lest I should have sorrow upon sorrow. (**Philippians 2:27**)

I am free from the bondage of fear and death.

And deliver them who through fear of death were all their lifetime subject to bondage. (**Hebrews 2:15**)

I am strengthened to walk God's path.

Wherefore lift up the hands which hang down, and the feeble knees; And make straight paths for your feet, lest that which is lame be turned out of the way; but let it rather be healed. (**Hebrews 12:12-13**)

Do You Know Jesus?

Romans 10:9 tells us, "That if thou shalt confess with thy mouth the Lord Jesus, and shalt believe in thine heart that God hath raised him from the dead, thou shalt be saved."

If Jesus Christ is not yet your Savior and Lord, you can pray this prayer to invite Him into your life.

Father God,

I acknowledge that I am a sinner and cannot save myself.

I believe Jesus came to pay for my sins.

I am sorry for my wrongdoings and ask for forgiveness.

I believe Jesus is Your Son, Who died and was buried but rose again after three days, conquering death and hell.

I am grateful that I am no longer condemned to death but have received the gift of eternal life through Jesus.

I believe the blood of Jesus cleanses me and makes me whole.

By faith, I accept Your forgiveness and love.

Jesus, I invite You to be my Savior and Lord, and I ask the Holy Spirit to guide me in Your ways.

Please fill me with Your presence and power, and help me live for You.

Thank You for Your love, mercy, and grace.

In Jesus' name,

Amen.

If you've just prayed this prayer for the first time, I encourage you to connect with other believers by joining a local church. Welcome to the family of Christ!

Can You Help?

We appreciate feedback and love hearing what readers have to say. Your input helps to make subsequent versions of this book and future books better.

Please leave an honest book review. Consider sharing your favorite quote or including a photo!

Stay up-to-date with new releases by visiting www.SallieDawkins.com.

More from this Publisher

- Identity in Christ: 100 Scriptures and Affirmations to Build Confidence

- 311 Questions Jesus Asked

- Spirit World Truths from God's Word

- God's Promises of Abundance for Healing

- Complete in Christ: Discovering Identity, Provision, and Purpose within God's Word

- God's Wisdom for Wealth: Flouring in Family & Business

- You Can Hear the Voice of God Through All Your Spiritual Senses

- You Can Know the Heart of God for Your Life

- You Can Share the Love of God with Others

- The Awakening Christian: Complete Series

- Maggie's Legacy: Lessons in Spiritual Obedience Learned from My Border Collie

Made in United States
Cleveland, OH
16 May 2025

16945365R00063